Rose Petal Jam

Flowers

and What They Are

by Mary Elting

illustrated by

Carl and Mary Hauge

Prepared under the editorial direction of
Dr. J. F. Stauffer, Professor of Botany,
The University of Wisconsin.

WHITMAN PUBLISHING COMPANY
Racine, Wisconsin

Contents

Copyright © 1961 by Whitman Publishing Company
All Rights Reserved

Library of Congress Catalog Card Number: 61-9974

Printed in the U.S.A.

Long Ago ✳✳✳✳✳

Kings and rulers long ago made some strange laws about a little blue flower called the autumn crocus that blooms in many a garden at the end of summer. Off came your head if you were caught stealing even one of the small brown knobs from which the autumn crocus grew. That was in the country of Syria.

In England it was once against the law for ladies to color their hair with a yellow dye made from this same flower. Weavers were not allowed to tint linen sheets with

9

it either. The dye that caused all this fuss is called saffron. It comes from tiny golden threads at the center of the crocus flower that pops out of the ground in the fall, instead of in the spring as other crocuses do.

People in the old days used saffron for other things besides dye. Rich men bought it to flavor their food. Sick people bought it to treat stomach-ache and measles. Since nearly a hundred thousand flowers were needed to make a pound of saffron, men who had it to sell charged a high price. Traders grew wealthy from it. No wonder it was a crime to take even one crocus plant away from Syria.

According to old stories, many men wanted to steal the knob-like crocus bulbs. Finally an Englishman risked his life to get a few of them. At that time, six hundred years ago, religious pilgrims often went on foot through Syria to the Holy Land. The Englishman decided to dress up like one of the pilgrims and to carry a staff. It looked like every other pilgrim's staff, but it was hollow. In this secret container the pilgrim-pirate managed to hide some of the precious little crocus knobs. No one caught him, and he smuggled them out of Syria into England.

The autumn crocus grew well in England, but there never seemed to be enough saffron to satisfy King Henry VIII. He ate a great deal, and he loved the flavor of saffron in his food. So he made it a crime for ladies to use any of it to color their hair, and he forbade weavers to dip linen sheets in saffron dye. His excuse for this was that yellow sheets didn't show dirt and wouldn't get washed often enough. Henry himself seldom took a bath, but he was king and his word was law.

Saffron dye would be popular today except that modern chemical dyes are cheaper. Cooks still flavor food with the golden spice, but modern drugs have taken its place as a cure for diseases.

Long ago people raised all kinds of lovely flowers, not for beauty but for seasoning and medicine. Monks and magicians grew healing herbs and plants in their gardens. They used primrose flowers to flavor puddings and to treat headaches. Marigold petals went into meat sauce, cheese, and soup. They were also supposed to cure bad eyesight and work magic against poison and angry words.

You can find recipes in ancient cookbooks for day lily soup, for eggs scrambled with calves' brains and rose petals, for boiled cattail buds, for salad made with chopped onions and wisteria petals, for cowslip pudding, and for candied violets.

Pima Indians in Arizona still eat the yellow flowers of the cholla cactus. Hopi Indians make chewing gum from the sticky stems of the globe mallow flower. The roots of another mallow are used in marshmallow candy.

In fancy food stores you can sometimes buy an old-fashioned delicacy, rose petal jam. But as a rule sweet-smelling flowers now go into perfumes instead of food. When the ancients made a perfume, they often used it for medicine as well as scent. Lily of the valley perfume was prescribed for heart trouble, and if you rubbed some of it on your forehead, it was supposed to give you common sense.

A few modern medicines come from flowering plants—foxglove, monkshood, belladonna, and castor oil. The milky juice that flows from scratches in young poppy seed pods is made into a pain-killing drug. The leaves of the aloe are used in treating radium burns.

What's in a Name?

THE NAMES OF SOME FLOWERS are hundreds of years old. Others are new. The pretty blue flower that we call larkspur used to be lousewort because its seeds really did kill lice. Its modern name comes from its shape, which is supposed to look like the hind claw of a lark.

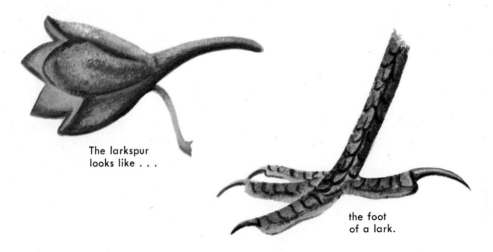

The larkspur looks like . . .

the foot of a lark.

Another handsome flower used to be called sowbread because pigs liked to eat its round, bulb-shaped roots. Most people now give it a fancier name—cyclamen, which means "circular." But scabiosa remains unchanged. It comes from a word that means "to scratch." The plant was once thought to cure itching skin.

Milkweed was named for the milky sap that oozes out of any wound in its stem. The sap dries to a sort of rubber which acts like a bandage when insects take nips out of the plant.

Nasturtium is a name that the ancient Romans made up. It means "nose twister." You'll know why if you eat a spicy leaf of the plant or one of its peppery seed pods.

Many, many flowers are named for things they resemble. For proof of this, take a look at beardtongue or—best of all—pussytoes.

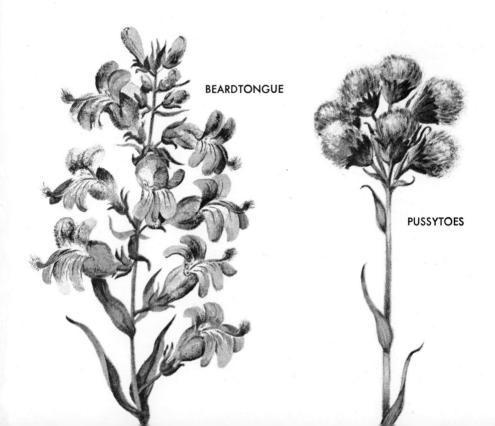

BEARDTONGUE

PUSSYTOES

How Does Your Garden Grow?

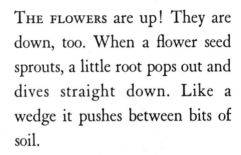

THE FLOWERS are up! They are down, too. When a flower seed sprouts, a little root pops out and dives straight down. Like a wedge it pushes between bits of soil.

Over the tip of the tender root is a cap that protects it from scratches. But what if the cap itself gets a scratch? All the better. Some of the tiny balloonlike cells of the cap are torn off. These act like the slippery balls of a roller bearing. Now the growing root is able to slide more easily through the earth.

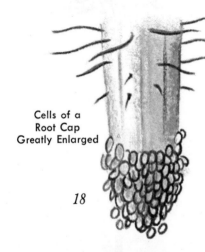

Cells of a
Root Cap
Greatly Enlarged

18

A slender bit of living plant can break through heavy soil. The secret of this strength is in tiny sacks called cells. A plant is entirely made of cells—millions of them. Growing cells fill up with liquid, mostly water. As a cell fills, it swells and gives a push. Of course, the push of one cell is so tiny that you can scarcely imagine it. But millions of cells, swelling up together, press hard enough to force solid earth to break.

While the root squirms downward, a stem pushes up. Some stems, like those of sweet peas, grow doubled over. Can you see how the arch in the stem gives it added strength for shouldering its way through earth?

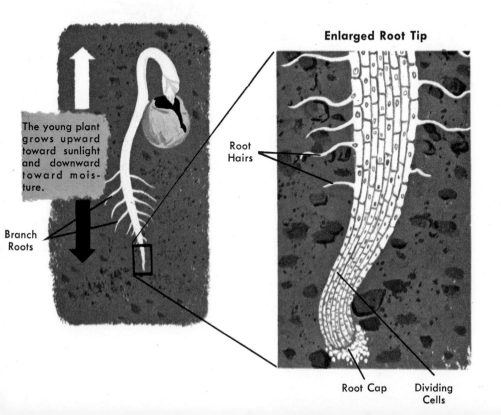

Enlarged Root Tip

The young plant grows upward toward sunlight and downward toward moisture.

Root Hairs

Branch Roots

Root Cap

Dividing Cells

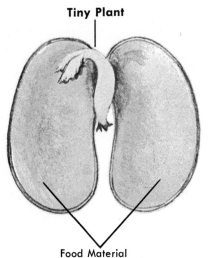

Tiny Plant

**Food Material
Stored in
"Seed Leaves"**

A plant needs food in order to live and grow. At first its tiny root and stem get nourishment from the seed. What happens when this little snack is gone? By then the new plant can make its own food.

Green leaves are the food makers. They get from the air and water and earth all the things they need to make food. Then, with the help of sunlight, green leaves turn these things into sugar—a type of food the plant uses for its nourishment.

The green in a plant is called *chlorophyll*. It holds the secret of the life of flowers—and what a deep secret that is! Scientists have learned how to send complicated rockets out into space to get information about the sun, but they haven't yet found out how sunlight and chlorophyll work together to make sugar. They do know this: during daylight hours sugar is formed faster than it can be moved out of the leaves. The extra sugar is changed into starch, but during the night this starch is changed back into sugar and moved back to the young parts of the plant, such as the tips of the stems, where it is used as food for growth.

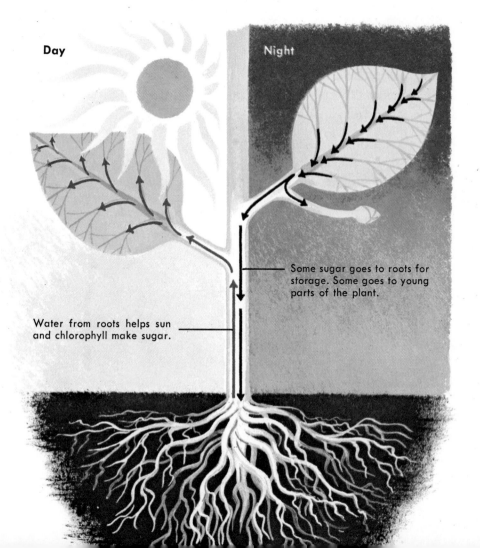

Day

Night

Some sugar goes to roots for storage. Some goes to young parts of the plant.

Water from roots helps sun and chlorophyll make sugar.

The Parts of a Flower and What They Do

Do YOU KNOW A FLOWER when you see one? That's a tricky question. Before answering, you'd better find out just what to look for. The diagram shows all the parts of a plain, simple flower. Use it as a guide when you go exploring among the other pictures.

Look for the petals first. Rose, hollyhock, poppy—those are easy. The bluebell's petals join together making a tube, and you'll find other tube flowers, too. Now the fun starts. The sweet pea's bonnet, the little elephant's head, and each pair of Dutchman's breeches hanging on the clothesline— all these odd shapes are really petals, too.

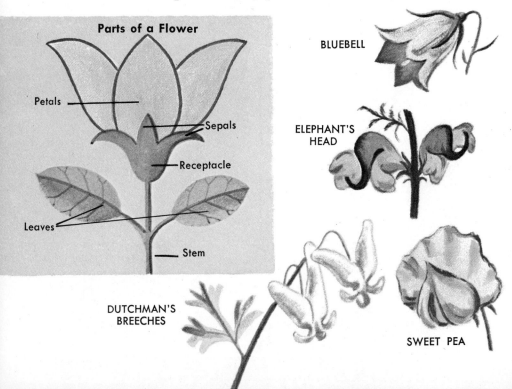

Parts of a Flower

Petals
Sepals
Receptacle
Leaves
Stem

BLUEBELL

ELEPHANT'S HEAD

DUTCHMAN'S BREECHES

SWEET PEA

The daisy belongs to a special group. In fact, you might call it a *daisies,* because each one is made of many little flowers. What's more, each daisy head combines flowers of two completely different types. The ones in the middle are called disk flowers. Those around the edges are ray flowers. Although each ray looks like a plain, ordinary petal, it really is a separate and distinct flower. The pictures show a few other flowers in this large family of two-in-ones.

DAISY

SUNFLOWER

ZINNIA

CHRYSANTHEMUM

23

Try hunting for *sepals* next. You'll have no trouble recognizing the hearty green ones that look almost like leaves either single or joined into a tube. But only an expert can tell sepals from petals in a columbine or fuchsia or delphinium. And the sepals of an iris or orchid look more like petals than the petals themselves.

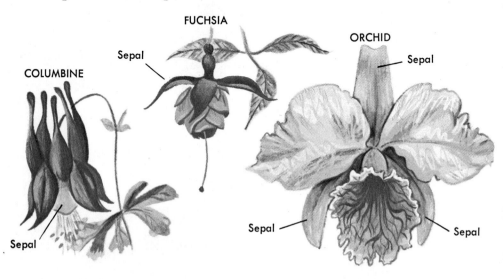

FUCHSIA
Sepal

COLUMBINE

Sepal

ORCHID
Sepal

Sepal

Sepal

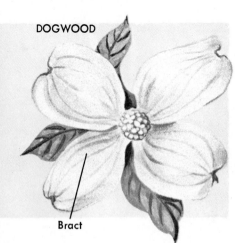

DOGWOOD

Bract

Does a dogwood flower have large pale petals? Or are they sepals? They're neither. The real flowers cluster together in the middle. Around them grow leaves that have changed their shape and color so that they look like petals. They are called *bracts*.

The poinsettia may have scarlet, pink, or white bracts.

You have to be a real flower detective to figure the last one out. The poinsettia's crimson bracts surround a little group of flowers. Each flower is shaped like a pot with a spout from which a syrupy liquid drips. A little ball dangles over one side of the pot. This will one day turn into seed.

The inside parts of a flower are sometimes as easy to recognize as fingers and thumbs. Let's start with the blossom of a sour cherry, which is a simple one.

At the very center stands a bottle-shaped part called the *pistil*. Inside the pistil is a little sack. This is the *ovule*. If all goes well, it will turn into a seed. Around the pistil stands a crowd of *stamens,* and on top of each one sits a little container full of yellow dust called *pollen*.

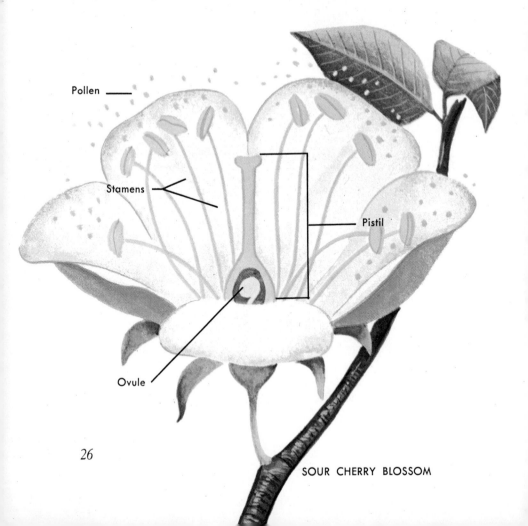

Pollen

Stamens

Pistil

Ovule

SOUR CHERRY BLOSSOM

Let's see how this simple arrangement works. Grains of pollen fall from stamen to pistil. Each pollen grain then sends out a long, slender tube. The tube pushes quickly down through the pistil, reaches the ovule, and joins with it. Now the ovule can turn into a seed. That's the story. Ovule plus pollen equals seed.

The seeds of some plants won't develop unless the ovule in one flower gets pollen from stamens in another of the same kind. Wind often spreads pollen from one of these flowers to another.

But some flowers have pollen that is heavy or sticky or difficult for the wind to get at. These have complicated arrangements, as you will see on the next page.

Ovule + Pollen = Seed

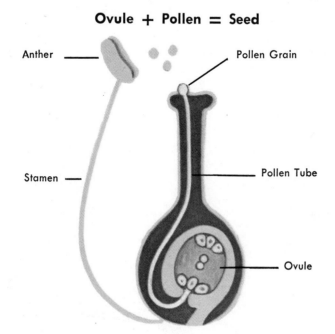

Anther

Pollen Grain

Stamen

Pollen Tube

Ovule

Bees often carry pollen from stamens to pistils. Some of the flowers they pollinate have parts that are arranged in surprising ways. The salvia blossom is a regular booby trap. When a bee pokes her head inside the flower, she pushes open a door. The door works a lever that moves the stamen, and down falls a shower of pollen from the stamen onto the bee's back. In the next salvia that she enters, her back rubs against the pistil, and so the pollen is spread.

A bee carries pollen from one
blossom to another.

A bee visits flowers to get nectar, a sweet syrup that oozes out around the base of the pistil. Nectar also serves as bait that lures humming birds, moths, and butterflies from one sweet meal to another. All of these carry away from a flower a few grains of pollen to leave wherever they take the next sip.

Some flowers have no nectar. What bait brings insects to them? Their pollen often does the trick. And no wonder, for pollen is coated with a kind of sweet gelatin that some insects eat. Bees collect it in lumps on their back legs and carry it home to their hives. Some of this loot rubs off as the insect goes from flower to flower, and so the pollen is spread.

Each flower has pollen grains of its own particular design. With a magnifying glass you can see what some of them look like. Hibiscus and four-o'clock are the largest. Most of the others are so small that you have to use a microscope to see them.

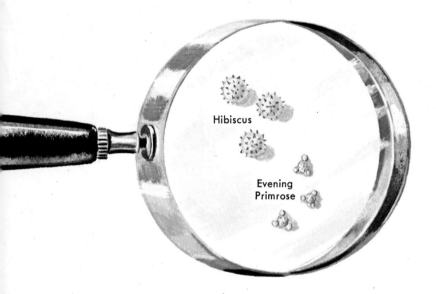

Hibiscus

Evening Primrose

**Pollen Grains Magnified
Many Times Their Actual Size**

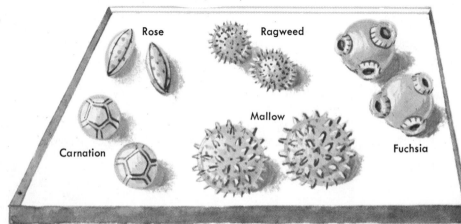

Rose

Ragweed

Mallow

Carnation

Fuchsia

Usually something more than luck guides a pollen-spreading insect toward a flower. Stripes on the lip of the iris clearly mark a landing field. The yellow center of a bluet is a nectar guide. Perfume brings a moth to a honeysuckle and tells a humming bird where to find a columbine. The scent of the bee balm attracts bees, and its bright red color is the guide for humming birds and butterflies.

IRIS

HONEYSUCKLE

All these tricky arrangements of landing fields and baited traps may seem mechanically perfect, and yet a flower isn't a machine. It lives and grows and creates more life through its seeds.

31

Night-Blooming Flowers

WOULD YOU EXPECT flowers to be waking up when you go to bed? Some do bloom at night. Many of them are light colored, which makes them easy to see in the dark. Some have a strong, sweet odor and are easy to smell.

It is important for these flowers to be seen or smelled in the dark because many of them are pollinated by night-flying moths. The nicotiana's perfume, for instance, lures the hawk moth to feed on the nectar in its deep tube-shaped flower. The moth sucks the nectar up through a drinking straw which is really its extra-long mouth. As the moth drinks, it gets dusted with pollen. Then off it goes, carrying the pollen to the next nicotiana where it stops for another sip.

The evening primrose also holds its nectar in a deep cup that only a moth with a long drinking tube can reach.

Some cactus plants have flowers that open only at night. One is the night-blooming cereus. It, too, is pollinated by a moth. Another cactus, the saguaro has white flowers that stay open at night. They are sometimes pollinated by long-nosed bats!

How Plants Travel

WHEN THE EARLY SETTLERS came to America, they brought seeds with them. In the strange new land a garden full of their favorite flowers reminded them of home. One man even got homesick for the old familiar weeds. He sent back to Europe for some weed seeds, and that's how Queen Anne's lace jumped across the Atlantic Ocean.

But flowers traveled long before people thought of gardens. Seeds have been moving over the earth for millions of years, and each flower has developed its own seed-

The pods of wild geraniums and touch-me-nots are made of thin strips that work like tightly stretched springs. As a ripe pod dries, it shrinks, till suddenly the strips break loose from one end. Each one coils up with such force that it flings a seed into the air.

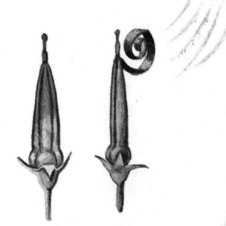

Wild Geranium Pod

Touch-Me-Not Pod

Lupine Pod

Some lupines have pods that burst with a violent spiral twist. There are other plants that spit or blow out their seeds. Each one of these marvelous plant-machines scatters the seeds for next year's flowers a few feet or a few yards away. And so, little by little, plants travel over the earth.

 *Flowers From Hidden Stems*

FLOWERS GROW FROM SEEDS. Then seeds grow from flowers. What about tulips? Did you ever see a tulip seed? Did you ever see anybody plant one? Probably not, but tulips do have seeds. It just happens that it is much easier to grow good tulip flowers from bulbs. That's true of the daffodil, hyacinth, and narcissus, too.

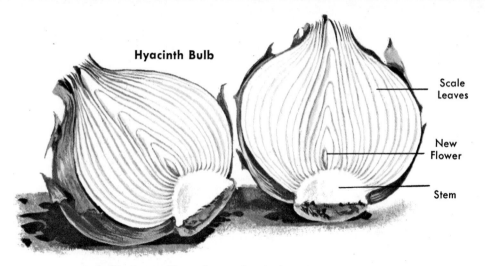

Hyacinth Bulb

Scale Leaves

New Flower

Stem

A bulb is really a large bud that has grown on a stem underground. If you cut a bulb down through the middle, you will see that it is a tight little package. It has all the parts of a flower wrapped up inside coat after coat of leaves. At the bottom of this flower package is a little nub of a thing that is actually a stem, though it doesn't look like any stem you are used to seeing.

The layers of tightly folded leaves that grow from this nub unfold when the earth warms up in the spring. The ready-made parts of a tulip push through the ground and burst into bloom. During the summer a new bulb— or maybe several—will form on the little underground stem, ready to grow next year.

Growing Tulip Bulb

Foliage Leaves

A gladiolus grows from an underground stem. So does a crocus. But this stem does not have a bud package attached to it. The outside looks somewhat like a bulb, but inside it is very different, and it is called a *corm*. If you cut a corm open you'll

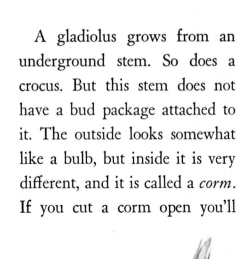

GLADIOLUS

Gladiolus Corm

Scale
Leaves

A Corm,
Split Open

find no tiny flowers wrapped around with leaves. The corm is solid all the way through. In the ground, lumpy little corms grow out of the big one. Each of these will sprout next year.

40

LILY OF THE VALLEY

Iris and cattail and lily of the valley also grow from underground stems, but they multiply in a different way. The stems of these plants grow sideways in the earth. Every once in a while a bud appears on the stem. Then up goes a shoot to form leaves and flowers.

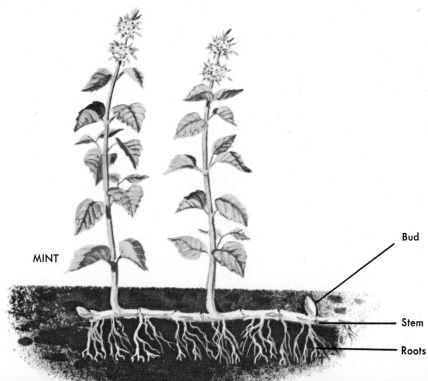

MINT

Bud

Stem

Roots

Watch Out!

IT SEEMS HARD TO BELIEVE that a flower is ever dangerous. But some can poison you, and it's a good idea to know about them.

Worst of the lot is the trumpet-shaped Jimson weed. Unfortunately it looks very much like its harmless, pretty cousin the petunia. Another wild poisonous relative is the henbane. Never put either of these in your mouth.

JIMSON WEED

PETUNIA

OLEANDER

Some gardeners keep the oleander as a house plant in winter and set it outside in a pot or tub during warm weather. Its flowers, leaves, and stem are very poisonous. Don't even touch them.

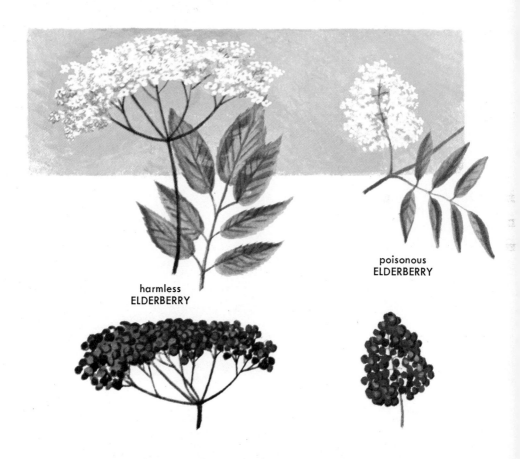

harmless
ELDERBERRY

poisonous
ELDERBERRY

There are two kinds of elder, both with white flowers. On one the flowers grow in a flat-topped cluster. They are harmless and so are the dark blue berries. The other has flowers that grow in rounded clusters. Its berries are bright red. Both the flowers and berries of this elder can give you a bad stomach-ache.

The best rule is, don't nibble on *any* flowers, seeds, stems, leaves, or unfamiliar berries.

From Forest and Jungle

IN EARLY SPRING you'll find the purple-and-brown hoods of skunk cabbages in the woods. Other members of this strange family live in the jungle where they grow to gigantic size. Their smell, like the odor of spoiled meat, attracts flies that carry pollen from one to another.

The AMORPHO-PHALLUS TITANUM cone may grow to a height of five or six feet.

GIANT RAFFLESIA

Jungle flies swarm around the great rafflesia, too. Its flowers are three feet across, with pink petals that turn dark and tough like huge flaps of leather.

The Dutchman's-pipe lures flies with its odor and holds them in traps made of curving hairs. After a fly buzzing around inside has pollinated the flower, these hairs wither and droop, and the prisoner goes free.

Odd, lovely jungle orchids used to be treasured and hoarded like jewels. In the days before scientists learned how to grow the flowers from seeds, orchid hunters roamed all over the world getting rare new plants for collectors. Moccasin flowers and lady's-slippers in our woods belong to the orchid family. People have picked so many of them that they really are becoming rare. If you find one, keep it a secret and leave it where it is.

MOCCASIN FLOWER

LADY'S-SLIPPER

THE STAR-SHAPED FLOWER of this pitcher plant grows among a cluster of very special leaves. Each leaf, folded into a sort of vase or pitcher, acts like a combination trap and stomach! If an insect blunders into the pitcher, it can't crawl out. It is trapped by curving, downward-pointing hairs. Strong juices ooze from the inside surface of the leaf, and before long they digest the insect, except for its hard outer covering.

STAR-SHAPED PITCHER PLANT

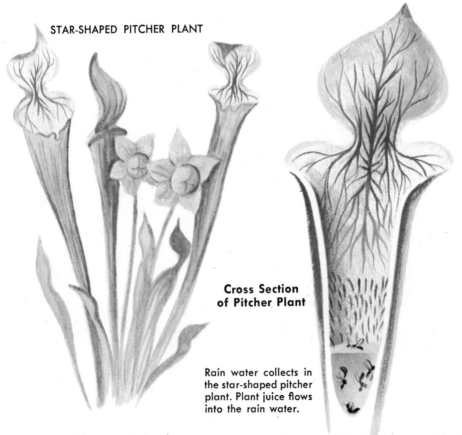

**Cross Section
of Pitcher Plant**

Rain water collects in
the star-shaped pitcher
plant. Plant juice flows
into the rain water.

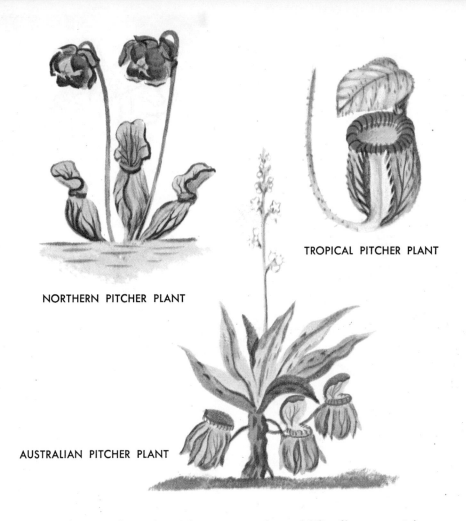

NORTHERN PITCHER PLANT

TROPICAL PITCHER PLANT

AUSTRALIAN PITCHER PLANT

Other pitcher plants have traps shaped like fat pots with lids. These dangle from the tips of the leaves, and they are often as beautifully colored as flowers.

Many other plants feed on animal life. Scientists call them *carnivorous,* which means "meat eating." All of them can get along perfectly well without their meat food, but they do grow larger when they have it.

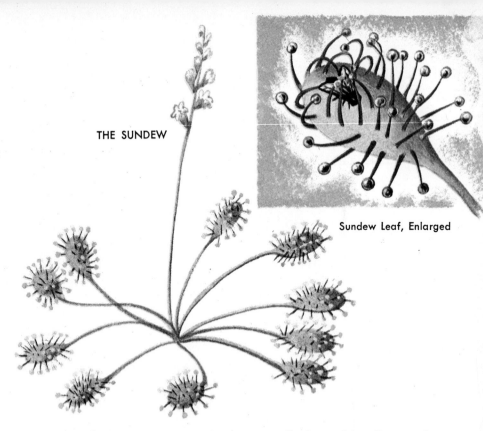

THE SUNDEW

Sundew Leaf, Enlarged

Search in a swamp and you may find a white flowered insect-eater that has leaves covered with little bristlelike arms. At the end of each arm gleams a drop of very sticky fluid which gives the plant its name—sundew. When a fly gets stuck to one of these drops, neighboring hairs bend over and touch the captive. Their sticky drops suffocate it and digest it, too.

What makes the arms bend? Actually they grow, but only on the side that's away from the fly. This unequal lengthening pushes the tips over and down. The wiggling of the trapped insect acts as a trigger that starts the growth.

Venus's-flytrap digests hamburger, flies, or ants. A sweet juice on the leaves acts as insect bait. Each leaf is hinged in the middle so that it can fold shut, and it is dotted with small sensitive hairs. When anything touches the hairs, they flash a message to the hinge which snaps the trap. Scientists believe that a tiny electric current carries the message, but they haven't yet discovered exactly how it works.

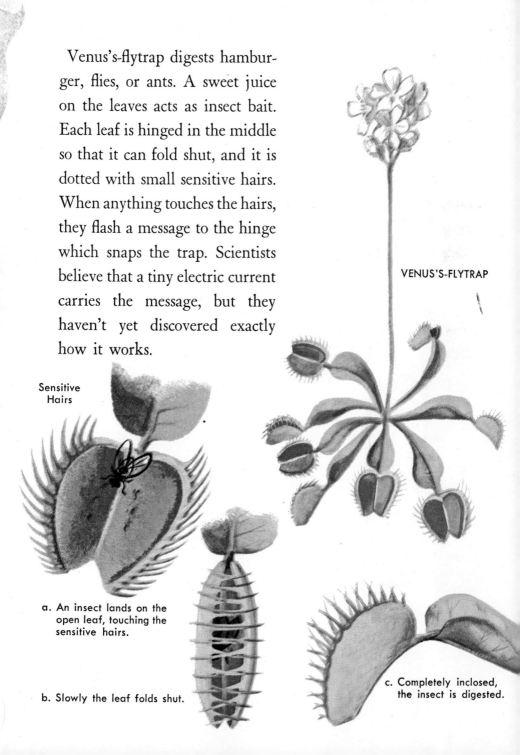

VENUS'S-FLYTRAP

Sensitive
Hairs

a. An insect lands on the open leaf, touching the sensitive hairs.

b. Slowly the leaf folds shut.

c. Completely inclosed, the insect is digested.

MORNING-
GLORY

THE GARDEN THAT SEEMS SO QUIET is full of great activity. Flower buds open. Leaves unfold. Vines climb.

Some vines go upward in a spiral. For example, the morning-glory climbs round and round a stake or wire, hugging it for support. When there is nothing else to climb, two morning-glories wind round each other.

Some climbers don't have spiraling stems. They get support only from slender, wiry tendrils that grow out of the stem and coil around any small thing they touch. You can see how they work if you watch a gourd plant for only two or three minutes. Put a stick in the ground so that it touches one of the plant's young tendrils. Right in front of your eyes the tendril will wind itself around the stick.

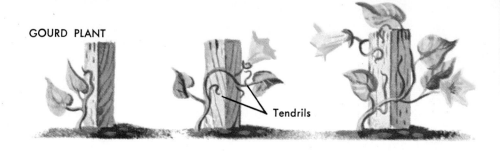

GOURD PLANT

Tendrils

A California poppy's activity starts after sunrise. Its petals unfold and spread wide. They close again at night, and any dew that forms will wet only the outside of the flowers. What happens if the inside gets wet? The pollen is likely to spoil, and then there will be no seeds.

CALIFORNIA POPPY

A Drooping
BUTTERCUP

Many flowers close not only at night but also before a rain. Some fold up even when the sky is cloudy. And the closed gentian tightens its petals if the sun merely spends a few moments behind a cloud.

Buttercups move in another way that protects their pollen from rain. Their heads suddenly droop. Petals become umbrellas!

The flowers of the peanut plant are active *after* they have been pollinated. First they droop. Next they drop their petals. Then the tip of the stalk turns downward and burrows into the earth. Underground, new peanuts develop in the pod that the tip of the stalk has buried.

PEANUT PLANT

Does the peanut flower *plan* to bury a pod so that seeds will be sure to grow? Does a poppy take a look at the weather and *decide* to close up because of rain? In other words, can flowers *think*?

Plants are living things, of course, but the fact is they can't plan or think or choose what they're going to do. Their tendency to move is built into the seeds they come from. Whatever makes a flower climb or burrow or open and close is there from its very beginning.

A CACTUS WITHOUT SPINES —this was a thing that didn't exist until a remarkable man decided to invent it. His name was Luther Burbank, and he loved to do things other people thought were impossible.

Burbank knew that seeds from any plant usually grow into new plants that are almost exactly like their parents. But not always. Sometimes a flower will be bigger than its parents, or smaller, or it will have petals or some other part that's different. Burbank watched for such things in his huge gardens. When he found an unusual plant, he saved it to see what kind of "plant children" it would have.

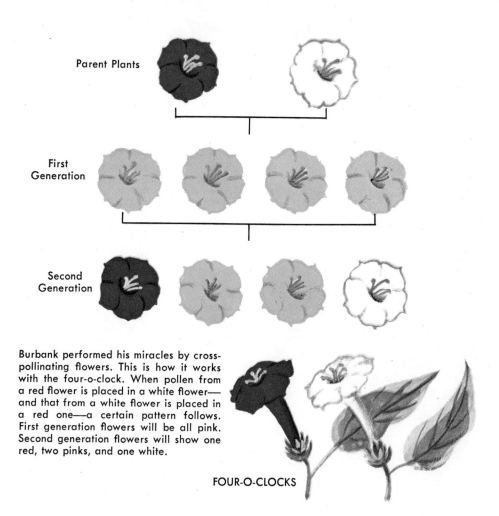

Parent Plants

First Generation

Second Generation

Burbank performed his miracles by cross-pollinating flowers. This is how it works with the four-o-clock. When pollen from a red flower is placed in a white flower—and that from a white flower is placed in a red one—a certain pattern follows. First generation flowers will be all pink. Second generation flowers will show one red, two pinks, and one white.

FOUR-O-CLOCKS

One of Burbank's favorite flowers was the calla, but it had a disagreeable smell. He kept wishing he could do something about it. Then one day, in a great bed of the flowers, he caught a whiff of sweet new perfume. Somewhere among the masses of callas was a freak with a delicious smell!

Burbank dropped to his knees and crawled up and down the rows. He sniffed at hundreds, thousands, of blossoms. At last he found the one he wanted, and he set it apart. From that one sweet-scented freak he developed the perfumed callas that you buy in a flower shop today.

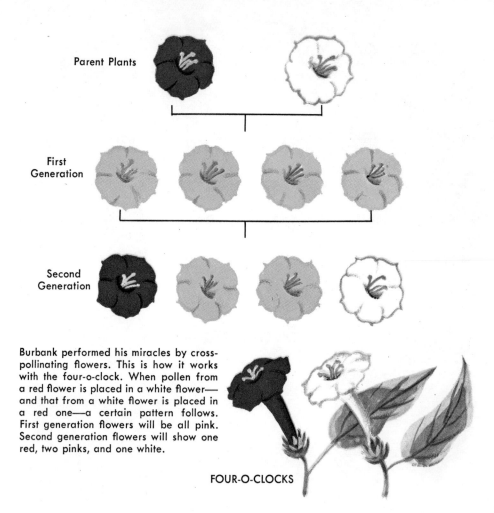

Parent Plants

First Generation

Second Generation

Burbank performed his miracles by cross-pollinating flowers. This is how it works with the four-o-clock. When pollen from a red flower is placed in a white flower—and that from a white flower is placed in a red one—a certain pattern follows. First generation flowers will be all pink. Second generation flowers will show one red, two pinks, and one white.

FOUR-O-CLOCKS

One of Burbank's favorite flowers was the calla, but it had a disagreeable smell. He kept wishing he could do something about it. Then one day, in a great bed of the flowers, he caught a whiff of sweet new perfume. Somewhere among the masses of callas was a freak with a delicious smell!

People from all over the world asked Luther Burbank to help them solve problems. A rancher who lived in a very dry part of Australia had trouble raising enough feed for his cattle. He wanted a big, juicy plant that would grow well in almost desert country. Something like a prickly pear would be good—if it had no prickles.

Burbank said he thought he could make a spineless cactus, and he did just that. After a while he shipped the rancher a new prickly pear cactus that had a smooth skin.

It takes a great deal of time and patience to change flowers and develop new ones. Plantsmen still work much as the pioneer Burbank did. But scientists are also experimenting with faster ways of making changes. They shoot X rays at seeds before putting them in the ground.

X rays cause changes in seeds. Plants that grow from X-rayed seeds are often quite different from their parents. If you want to see how this works, you can buy some X-rayed seeds from a flower grower and plant them in your garden. You may get some dwarfs or giants, new colors, or strange shapes never seen before.

What made Burbank's first perfumed calla appear all of a sudden? Why do X rays create new kinds of flowers? Scientists know part of the answer to these questions. Someday, somebody will puzzle out the whole answer. Perhaps that somebody may be you!

WHAT IS MOON MILK?

HOW DO ENGINES WORK?

HOW DEEP CAN DIVERS GO?

Whitman
Learn About Books

THE MICROSCOPE AND A HIDDEN WORLD TO EXPLORE *Irene S. Pyszkowski*

Learn how man discovered the hidden world of the invisible. Find out how microscopes are used by detectives, scientists, doctors, and how it is possible to see tiny living things all around us.

ASTRONOMY—OUR SOLAR SYSTEM AND BEYOND *Robert I. Johnson*

Find out about the planets and moons that circle our star, the Sun. Look at actual photographs of craters on the moon, giant tornadoes on the Sun, and exploding stars millions of miles away from us.

ADVENTURES IN SCIENCE *Charles D. Neal*

Experiments to be done at home show how sound, heat, and light travel . . . why lemon juice can be used to write secret messages . . . why a can heated in just the right way crumples when it cools—and much more.

FIND OUT! FIRST STEP TO THE FUTURE *Dr. Dan Q. Posin*

Have you ever wondered how a telescope works? Or how storms happen? Or how the big electronic brains work? Or how atoms join to make all things on Earth—and in space? Dr. Posin has the answers!

ROCKETS TO EXPLORE THE UNKNOWN *Don E. Rogers*

Learn how rockets, and cannons—and bicycles!—are all a little alike. Find out how rockets work, and how they are being designed to fly faster and farther, to carry man out into unknown space.

BOOKS IN THE LEARN ABOUT SERIES

THE AIRPORT, OUR LINK TO THE SKY
Robert Sidney Bowen

ANIMALS OF THE FIELD AND FOREST
Mina Lewiton

BIRDS AROUND US
Marjorie Stuart

FLOWERS AND WHAT THEY ARE
Mary Elting

TREES AND HOW THEY GROW
Katharine Carter

OUR EARTH, WHAT IT IS
Frederick H. Pough

ROCKS AND WHAT THEY TELL US
Lester del Rey

RIVERS, WHAT THEY DO
Nancy Larrick and Alexander Crosby

PHYSICS, ITS MARVELS AND MYSTERIES
Dr. Daniel Q. Posin

THE BIG BUILDERS
E. Joseph Dreany

TURN TO THE SEA
Athelstan Spilhaus

CAVES AND THEIR MYSTERIES
James McClurg

ENGINES, PROGRESS AND POWER
Don E. Rogers

YOUR BODY
Harry Swartz, M.D.